Marriage and Family
Basic Training Course

Dr. Nicolas Ellen

Marriage and Family
Basic Training Course

Readers may order copies by visiting www.mycounselingcorner.com

Published and Printed By Expository Counseling Center
Houston, Texas

Unless otherwise noted, scripture references are taken from the New American Standard Bible. © The Lockman Foundation, 1960, 1962, 1963, 1968, 1971, 1972, 1973, 1975, 1977.

Publisher's Cataloging in Publication

Ellen, Nicolas: *Marriage and Family*
1. Counseling 2. Psychology 3. Christianity 4. Discipleship

ISBN 978-0-9779691-7-3

TABLE OF CONTENTS

MARRIAGE AND FAMILY

MARRIAGE AND FAMILY

(Section One)

THE BIBLICAL DEFINITION OF A FAMILY

I. The Premise of the Family as God Intended

  A. The family was intended to consist of a man and a woman who are committed to one another under God.
  B. This man and woman are to live together as Husband and Wife with children who are related by birth or adoption through a mother/father relationship or by parentage of a biblical marriage to each other and and managed by the Father/Husband to glorify God in all aspects of life (Genesis 1:26-31, 2:18, 21-25, 18: 19).
  C. The family is to provide companionship, nurture, discipline, and training in righteousness so that all would be able to live a life that is pleasing to God and beneficial to society.
  D. The family was intended to be the means by which God reflects the nature of His relationship with His people.
      1. Husband/wives: Ephesians 5:22-23;
                         Revelations 19:9
      2. Father/child: Deuteronomy 32:6-18;
                        Romans 8:12-17;
                        2 Corinthians 6:16-18;
                        John 1:12; 1 John 3:16

II. The Priority of the Family to our Social Structure

  A. The family is the basic building block of every other social unit or institution (Genesis 1:26-28).
  B. The family was the only entity on earth commanded to be fruitful and multiply (Genesis 1:28).
  C. Distortions and deficiencies in our families will produce distortions and deficiencies in every other human institution; therefore, the family has a large influence on society.

III. The Picture of the Family as God Intended

A. To be a place of companionship where a husband and wife work together to accomplish God's will living out a covenant marriage before God and others (Genesis 2:18-25).
B. To be a place where the husband is a servant leader to the wife and family in all aspects of the family (Ephesians 5:22-6:4).
C. To be a place where the wife supports her husband and family in all aspects of the family (Proverbs 31:10-31).
D. To be a place where children are born and valued (Psalm 127:4-5).
E. To be a place where the will of God is taught and lived out from generation to generation resulting in Christian character, conduct, and conversation being developed accordingly (Deuteronomy 4:1-9, Luke 6:40-45, Titus 2:1-5).
F. To be a place where children are taught to obey and respect God and all other authority through discipline and instruction from the Word of God (Ephesians 6:4).
G. To be a place where mothers and fathers are honored through the wisdom of their children (Proverbs 10:1).
H. To be a place where people are an asset and not a liability to each other resulting in bearing burdens and meeting needs of one another (Psalm 128:1-6).
I. To be a place where people live by the commandments of God from the heart and not allow the traditions of the culture or other family members to hinder resulting in the fruit of God being produced by all (James 3:13-18, John 15:8).

THE PURPOSE FOR MARRIAGE
(Genesis 2:15-25)

I. God designed marriage for *Companionship* (Genesis 2:15-18)

    A. Marriage was designed so that man would not be alone (Genesis 2:18).

    B. Marriage was designed so that man would not be alone in fulfilling God's plan (Genesis 2:18).

    C. Marriage was designed for man and woman to be lifelong partners that would meet genuine needs of one another, and satisfy legitimate desires of one another for life as priority above everyone else and all things except for God Himself (1 Corinthians 7:33-34).

II. God designed marriage for *Co-laboring* (Genesis 2:15-18)

    A. Marriage was designed to provide man with a woman to assist him in his God-given responsibilities (Genesis 2:15-23).

    B. Marriage was designed to demonstrate how man and woman could work together as a team in fulfilling God's commandment accordingly (Genesis 1:26-28).

    C. Marriage was designed to show how man and woman are to work together in a union (Genesis 2:15-23, 1 Corinthians 11:8-12).

III. God designed marriage for *Cleaving* (Genesis 2:18-24)

    A. Man and Woman are called to come together in marriage as a family unit separate from mother and father.

    B. Man and Woman are called to come together in marriage and build a foundation based on their new family, not their original family.

    C. Man and Woman are called to come together to work on oneness in marriage.

IV. God designed marriage for *Completion* (Genesis 2:18-24)

    A. Marriage was designed so that man and woman can help each other come to know Christ intimately.

    B. Marriage was designed so that man and woman can help each other become like Christ ultimately.

    C. Marriage was designed so that man and woman can help each other be useful to Christ practically, resulting in fulfilling their God-given purposes.

V. God designed marriage for *Complementing* (Ephesians 5:25-33)

    A. Marriage was designed to reveal how Christ relates to the Church (Ephesians 5:23-33).

    B. People are to see how Christ loved the Church as they see how a man loves his wife (Ephesians 5:25).

    C. People are to see how the Church is to submit to Christ as they see how a woman submits to her husband (Ephesians 5:22).

Understanding Manhood

I. <u>The Definition of a Male</u>: (*zakar* /zaw·**kawr**/) One who was created by God as a material and immaterial being, with a unique DNA, 1X chromosome, and the physical distinctive of a penis and testicles for a particular function and purpose in the culture alongside and distinct from a female (woman) and all other creations of God. (Genesis 1:27)

    A. In most cases men are born with a penis and testicles. In the event there is either a void of or having an addition to his normal organs, a chromosome test should verify his gender.

II. <u>The Definition of Manhood</u>: (*andrizomai* [to act manly])[1] - the mindset, manner, and movement that correspond distinctly to a male in form and function.[2] (1Corinthians 16:13)

    A. Manhood is also tied to men who develop to the fullness of their being in courage- the mental and moral strength to resist opposition, handle danger, or endure hardship while operating in a mindset, manner and movement that is distinctly male, glorifying to God and beneficial to others; to have firmness of mind and will in the face of danger or extreme difficulty while operating in a mindset, manner and movement that is distinctly male, glorifying to God and beneficial to others (1Corinthains 16:13).[3]

III. <u>The Duties of a Male</u>: The duties of a male correspond with how He was created by God from the beginning to function: (1 Corinthians 11: 1-3)

    A. Men are responsible for taking the lead in ***procreation on earth***-giving life through his seed to his wife only, to carry that life to birth so that mankind would reflect the character of God throughout the earth. (Genesis 1:26-30)

    B. Men are responsible for taking the lead in ***subduing the earth***- to govern the earth i.e. stewardship, management, control, and order according to the will of God. (Genesis 2:15,19-20, 1:26-30)

    C. Men are responsible for taking the lead in ***dominion of the earth***- being a servant leader over creation resulting exercising his authority, influence,

---

[1]Kittel, Gerhard ; Friedrich, Gerhard ; Bromiley, Geoffrey William: *Theological Dictionary of the New Testament*. Grand Rapids, Mich. : W.B. Eerdmans, 1995, c1985, S. 59
[2]Ibid
[3]Merriam-Webster, Inc: *Merriam-Webster's Collegiate Dictionary*. Eleventh ed. Springfield, Mass. : Merriam-Webster, Inc., 2003 (definition of the word courage)

and strength, over creation and all who fall under his leadership for the glory of God and the good of creation[4] (Genesis 2:15, 19-20 1:26-30).

D. In essence men are to **procreate** with spouse only, **govern** within the realm of authority, influence and strength given by God, and **_lead_** within the realm of authority, influence, and strength given by God. (Genesis 2:15, 1:26-30, 1 Corinthians 11:1-3)

IV. **The Disciplines of Manhood**: Man's primary goal is not to relax; Man's primary goal is to work for the glory of God[5] Men were not called to follow the world's order but set things in order in all aspects of life to the Glory of God and the benefit of mankind.[6] Therefore, it is prudent for man to learn, live, and discipline himself around the Precepts and Plans of God. (Genesis 1:27, Genesis 2:15, 1Corinthians 11:1-3, Proverbs 14:8)

THE PRACTICE OF A HUSBAND

I. **Husbands are to love their wives (Ephesians 5:25-30)**

A. Meaning—to self sacrifice for the benefit, provision, welfare of his wife in all aspects of her life (Ephesians 5:25-31).
B. Member—to his wife (Ephesians 5:25-31).
C. Manner—as Christ loved the Church (Ephesians 5:25-31).
D. Motive—to help her to become Holy/Blameless; that she may function according to God's design (Ephesians 5:25-31).
E. Magnitude—to death (1John 3:16-18).
F. Manifestation—considering her interest, concerns, needs, desires, and making sure they are taken care of in the way that Christ would do it for the Church; relating with her socially, spiritually, emotionally, and sexually in a manner that benefits her and reflects the character of Christ; compensating for her weaknesses in ways that Christ would do it for the Church; leading and guiding her into spiritual maturity, helping her to be all of what God designed her to be in the way that Christ would do it for the Church; leading your wife as Christ would lead the Church in all aspects of the marriage (1 Peter 3:7, 1 Corinthians 7:33).

---

[4] Berg, Jim, The Pursuit of Manhood: Discovering the Journey and Joys of Biblical Masculinity (Greenville, SC: 2009), Syllabus from teaching), 8.

[5] Chanski, Mark, Manly Dominion: In A Passive-Purple Four Ball World (Merrick, NY: Calvary Press Publishing, 2004), 49-50.

[6] Dewitt, David, The Mature Man: Becoming a Man of Impact (Gresham, Oregon: Vision House Publishing Inc., 1994), 9-21.

Implications for Men

A. Men must manage the ***people*** within the garden God has placed them according to the commands of God.

B. Men must maintain and manage the ***possessions*** within the garden God has placed them according to the commands of God.

C. Men must maintain and manage the ***property*** within the garden God has placed them according to the commands of God.

D. Men must disengage from ***perpetrators*** that keep them from functioning within their God-given roles as commanded by God.

E. Men must distrust ***perspectives*** that keep them from functioning within their God-given roles as commanded by God.

F. Men must deny ***passions*** that keep them from functioning within their God-given roles as commanded by God.

Example of a Job description developed

POSITION TITLE: Husband (Head of Family)

PURPOSE OF THE POSITION: To lead, love, feed, watch over, protect and serve wife, and those of the Household (1Cor 11:3, Eph 5:25-27, 1Tim 5:8, John 13:1-17, 1John 3:16, Acts 20:28).

REPORTS TO: Jesus Christ, Elders, Accountability Couple

RELATES CLOSELY WITH: Wife, Mother, Father, Mother in Law and Father in Law

RESPONSIBLE FOR:
- Leading family in the direction designed by God for this family (Joshua 24:14-15).
- Setting an example for Godly living (Matthew 5:6, 1Timothy 4:16).
- Establishing a system for discipling the family to spiritual maturity (Ephesians 5:25-27,6:4, Hebrews 10:24, Proverbs 22:6, 1Corinthians 14:35).
- Providing financial provisions to meet the basic needs of the immediate family and household (1Timothy 5:8, 1John 3:16-19).
- Establishing guidelines and goals for every aspect of living in the home that are according to God's Standards and God's Design for the Family (1Timothy 3:4-5).
- Providing support and service to all members in the household in order that they may live out the purpose God designed for each individual in the household (Romans 12:9-13, Hebrews 3:12-13).
- Protecting the family against hurt, harm, and danger (1John 3:16, Acts 20:28).
- Providing sexual fulfillment to wife unconditionally (1Corinthians 7:1-5).

CONTINUING RESPONSIBILITIES:
- Assisting in handling household responsibilities (Philippians 2:3-4).
- Tracking the spiritual growth of the immediate family and household (John 21:15-17).
- Honoring, Praising, and Showing appreciation to my wife on a consistent basis (Proverbs 31:28, 1Peter 3:7).
- Establishing and providing opportunities for family fun, fellowship and travel (Acts 2:42, Hebrews 10:25).
- Seeking to constantly understand who my wife is and how to serve and honor her accordingly (1Peter 3:7).

Measurable Goals for the Position

- What life skills are being developed in my life and family?
- What needs am I meeting for my wife, children and others right now?
- What commitments am I keeping?
- What household responsibilities am I maintaining?
- What social events/hobbies have we been involved in?
- What trips have we taken?
- What level of spiritual maturity is found in my family?
- Who's burdens are we bearing and needs are we meeting for one another and those outside the family?
- What have I protected my family from?
- What financial provisions are being made for my family?
- How much debt are we going into?
- How much debt are we coming out of?
- What goals have we set and accomplished as a family /as individuals in the family?
- What souls have been saved as a result of our family?
- What lives have grown spiritually as result of our family?

Understanding Womanhood

I. <u>**The Definition of Female:**</u> [*nâqebah* /nek·ay·**baw**/] One who was created by God as a material and immaterial being, with a unique DNA, 2x chromosome, and the physical distinctive of a vagina, womb, ovaries and uterus for a particular function and purpose in the culture alongside and distinct from a male and all other creations of God. (Genesis 1:27)

    A. In most cases women are born with a vagina, womb, ovaries, and uterus. In the event there is a void of or having an addition to her normal organs, a chromosome test should verify her gender.

II. <u>**The Definition of Womanhood**</u>: The mindset, manner, and movement that all females were distinctly created and called by God to function in all aspects of life. (Genesis 2:18)

III. <u>**The Duties of a Female:**</u> The duties of a female correspond with how she was created by God from the beginning to function: (Genesis 2:18) *ézer kenegdo – A helper who is like a male or who is comparable in essence/being only – Gen.2:18*

    A. Women are responsible for supporting men in ***procreation on earth***- carrying the life implanted through the seed of her husband to birth so that mankind would reflect the character of God throughout the earth. (Genesis 1:26-30)

    B. Women are responsible for supporting men in ***subduing the earth***- support men in governing the earth i.e. stewardship, management, control, and order according to the will of God.(Genesis 2:15,19-20, 1:26-30)

    C. Women are responsible for supporting men in ***dominion of the earth***- supporting men in the overseeing the earth Genesis 2:15, 19-20 1:26-30)

    D. In essence women are to **procreate** with spouse only**, support** men and ***submit*** to men in the governance and leadership of creation within realm of their influence and position to the glory of God and the good of mankind (Genesis 2:15, 1:26-30, 1 Corinthians 11:1-3).

IV. <u>**The Disciplines of Womanhood**</u>: A women was not designed to take a man's place but to work alongside a man. A woman is to operate in such a manner whereby her talents, gifts, abilities corresponds or complements male headship. She is not operate in manner whereby she seeks to replace or be co-equal to male headship. Therefore, it is prudent for woman to learn, live, and discipline herself around the Precepts and Plans of God.

(Genesis 1:27, 2:18, 1Corinthians 11:1-3, Proverbs 14:8)

THE PRACTICE OF A WIFE

I. Wives are to submit to their husbands (Ephesians 5:22-24)

A. Meaning—to willingly follow the leadership of your husband; to willingly follow the instructions of your husband (Ephesians 5:22-24).

B. Member—to her own husband (1Peter 3:1-6).

C. Manner—as the Church submits to Christ the Lord; as if she were responding to Jesus Christ Himself (Ephesians 5:22-24).

D. Motive—out of respect for God's design (Ephesians 5:22-24).

E. Magnitude—in everything that is not sin including Preferences (Ephesians 5:22-24).

F. Manifestation—following her husband's leadership and directives in all that she does in the home and outside the home as unto the Lord; following her husband's leadership and directives in the raising of the children as unto the Lord; showing respect to her husband in all aspects of the marriage as unto the Lord; managing their home in ways that are in line with her husband's leadership and directives as unto the Lord; listening to and following through on the things that concern her husband that have been requested of her as unto the Lord (Titus 2:3-5, Proverbs 31:10-31, 1 Corinthians 7:34, 1 Peter 3:1-6).

Implications for Women

A. Women must *delight* in their position as coheirs with men before the throne of God.

B. Women must *develop* in the precepts of God in relation to all that God has for women to do in their position and practice established for them through the creation order.

C. Women must be *disciplined* in their practice of functioning within the role that God established through the creation order.

D. Women must *dismiss* the perspective that they are less than men because of the role God established for them through the creation order.

E. Women must be *devoted* to promoting their position and their practice ordained by God to other women so that God may be glorified through their position and practice.

F. Women must *discover* the pleasure that God brings to their lives as a result of living within the created order of God.

Example of a Job description developed

POSITION TITLE: Wife (Support of Family)

PURPOSE OF THE POSITION: To support and help her husband in various ways so that he may be and do all God designed for him (Genesis 2:18-22).

REPORTS TO: God, Husband, Church Leaders

RELATES CLOSELY WITH: Husband, Mother, Father, Mother in law and father in law

RESPONSIBLE FOR:
- Submitting to husband in every aspect of life as unto the Lord (Eph 5:23, Titus 2:3-5,1Peter 3:1)
- Helping her husband in those areas of his life where he is unable to function adequately (Genesis 2:18)
- Meeting his needs in every aspect of the Marriage (Philippians 2:3-4, 1Peter 4:10)
- Showing respect to her husband (Ephesians 5:33)
- Keeping the home inviting and orderly (Titus 2:3-5 Psalm 128:3 Proverbs 31:27)
- Assisting her husband in the raising of children (Titus 2:3-5, Psalm 128:3)
- Keeping herself beautiful inside and outside (1Peter 3:3-5)
- Providing sexual fulfillment to her husband unconditionally (1Corinthians 7:1-5)
- Using her skills, talents, gifts to support her husband and family as first priority (Proverbs 31:27, Psalm128:3, Titus 2:3-5)
- Being loyal, trustworthy, and dependable in attitude, action, and service to her husband in every aspect of the relationship (Proverbs 31:10-12)

Measurable Goals
- In what ways am I submitting to my husband?
- How am I using my strengths to compensate for my husband's weaknesses?
- What needs am I meeting of my husband?
- What ways am I showing respect to my husband?
- Am I keeping the home inviting and orderly?
- What ways am I helping my husband raise our children?
- What am I doing to keep myself attractive for my husband?
- Is my husband satisfied sexually by me?
- What gifts, talents, skills, and resources am I using to support my Husband/my family?

Marriage and Family

(Section Two)

The Pursuit of Oneness

I. The Definition of Oneness in Marriage

    A. A husband and wife becoming a team
    B. A husband and wife becoming a team that functions together
    C. A husband and wife becoming a team that functions together in such a way that produces edification and transformation of both as a result of the union

II. You must strive for Oneness in Intellectual Understanding

    A. A husband and wife must be able to have a common ground of understanding.
    B. Each must define their terms and develop a common ground and meaning of terms.
    C. There must be a sharing of ideas and a willingness to listen to ideas.
    D. There has to be a learning together of wisdom with each other.

III. You must strive for Oneness in Spiritual Growth

    A. There must be a joint commitment to study the Word of God and prayer.
    B. There must be a joint commitment to confessing and repenting of sin.
    C. There must be a joint commitment to bearing burdens and meeting needs.
    D. There must be a joint commitment to proclaiming the truth of God's Word as well as a maintaining of worship of our Lord in Spirit and Truth.

IV. You must strive for Oneness in Communication

    A. You must develop a common ground in perspective to communicate on a common level.

    B. You must develop a common ground in interpretation so understanding of communication can develop.

    C. You must develop a common ground in how to share ideas with each other.

    D. You must evaluate what you tend to believe about each other on a regular basis so that there will be a better interpretation of each other's words.

V. You must strive for Oneness in Aspirations

    A. You and your spouse should sit down and develop a mission statement based on God's design for marriage.

    B. You and your spouse should work in pursuing practical things you want to make happen in the marriage.

    C. You must develop objectives for the marriage that are based on biblical principles.

    D. You must create a process by which you both can pursue accomplishing what you want for the marriage that will honor God.

VI. You must strive for Oneness in Affection

    A. There must be an understanding of how to touch each other in ways that penetrates the soul and massages the emotions.

    B. You must learn how to touch each in a way that is physical without being sexual.

    C. Affection must be given in such a way that God is glorified and you and your spouse are edified.

    D. You must learn how to touch each other in such a way that both feel wanted and loved.

VII. You must strive for Oneness in Sexual Activities

    A. You must learn the sexual desires and passions of one another.

    B. You must practice these things frequently in marriage!

    C. As you learn the appetites and interest of one another there must be a commitment to satisfy the other accordingly.

    D. Both must be committed to sex with their spouse alone and allow themselves to be free sexually in the marriage.

VIII. You must strive for Oneness in Work Related Activities

    A. Decisions must be made as to if your wife will work or be a housewife.

    B. Strategies must be developed in supporting each other in whatever job each may have.

    C. A job's benefit and detriment should be determined by how it adds to or takes away from the marital relationship and bring glory or takes away glory from God's will for marriage.

    D. Work related activities should be pursued or rejected on the basis of how it impacts the marital relationship as God intended.

IX. You must strive for Oneness in Financial Management

    A. There must be a decision as to who will manage the money and how the money will be managed, as well as how the money will be spent.

    B. There has to be a redefining of values within the relationship as it relates to spending.

    C. There has to be a coming together on the balancing of check books.

    D. There has to be a coming together on how money will be saved and when the savings will be used.

X. You must strive for Oneness in Resolving Problems

    A. Problem solving must focus on finding solutions instead of rehearsing the problems.

    B. There must be an approach to dealing with problems that you both can develop that will move towards resolution instead of more fights.

    C. There needs to be a time to review the Scripture to understand God's perspective on the matter so that each can respond accordingly to the problems that will arise.

    D. You must develop a biblical view and process for resolving the problem that can be pursued as a team.

XI. You must strive for Oneness in Parenting

    A. There must be discussion and agreement on the issue of birth control. In other words, what do you believe the Bible has to say about it, and how will that be applied to your home?

    B. There must be discussion and agreement on the issue of discipline. How does the Bible say we are to discipline our children and are you both willing to work this out in the context of your family?

C. There has to be discussion and agreement on raising children or there will be a lot of arguing and debating.

D. All these discussions must be driven by God's precepts. If not, personal preferences on parenting will create division when they differ from one or the other.

XII. You must strive for Oneness in Ministry Service

A. You must understand how you and your spouse are gifted and help each other function in your gifts accordingly.

B. There needs to be an understanding of how God can use you and your spouse as a team in the service of His Kingdom.

C. As you understand each other, there must be an on how you will work as a team and how you will work as individuals in your service for God.

D. There should be an understanding between you and your spouse that serving others should not ever hinder serving each other.

XIII. You must strive for Oneness in Social Activities

A. Your social activities should primarily revolve around you and your spouse.

B. There should be a developing of a certain hobbies together.

C. There should be a showing of interest n the hobbies of your spouse.

D. A lot of leisure time should be spent together doing things together that each enjoys accordingly.

XIV. You must strive for Oneness in Friendships

A. It is important that friendship be a support and not sabotage the marital relationship.

B. You must develop mutual friendships while discussing how to maintain or minimize time spent with friends that are not mutual.

C. There should be more friends that you have together than you have apart.

XV. You must strive for Oneness in Fellowship with Extended Family

A. There must be a consideration as to how much time you will spend together with each other's family.
B. You must consider holidays and birthdays as well as leisure time in relation to extended family.
C. There should be a lot of consideration given to each other on the matter of extended family visitation.
D. No one should allow family members to take advantage of open doors to the home.

THE PRACTICE OF GIVING LOVE TO YOUR SPOUSE

I. The attitude of giving love to your spouse (Philippians 2:1-16)

    A. Consider your spouse's interest as being just as important as yours (Philippians 2:1-5)

    B. Focus on what God says above what your spouse thinks of you (Romans 12:1-3).

    C. Focus on what is best for your spouse, not what is good to you (1 Corinthians 13:5).

    D. Focus on how your spouse will benefit, not how much you have to sacrifice or what you can gain (1 Corinthians 13:5, 7).

II. The wisdom in giving love to your spouse (Proverbs 3:27-28)

    A. Give your spouse whatever he or she may need from you on a consistent basis (Proverbs3:27-28).

    B. Do not withhold providing what he or she may need from you because you are angry or disappointed with him or her (Proverbs 3:27-28).

    C. Give to your spouse without depending on your feelings but by your faith (Proverbs 3:27-28).

    D. Give to your spouse according to the Word of God as it relates to marriage and your relationship to God (Ephesians 5:22-33).

III. Expressions of love to express towards your wife (Ephesians 5:25-29)

    A. Make sacrifices that will help your wife become the woman God wants her to be (Ephesians 5:25-27).

    B. Provide for the physical needs of your wife in order to nourish and promote good health and strength (1 Timothy 5:8).

    C. Have tenderness and give affection to your wife (Ephesians 5:28-29).

    D. Live with your wife, seeking to understand her in order to live with her in a way that is God-honoring and beneficial to her (1Peter 3:7).

    E. Honor your wife—treat her as a prized possession; treat her as a valuable treasure (1 Peter 3:7).

    F. Avoid being bitter towards your wife (Colossians 3:19).

    G. Be available for your wife sexually as often as she desires (1 Corinthians 7:3-5).

IV. Expressions of love to express towards your husband (Ephesians 5:22-24, 33)

A. Submit to your husband in everything—except for any thoughts, words, or actions the Bible would define as sin (Ephesians 5:24).
B. Show respect to your husband (Ephesians 5:33).
C. Be a husband/lover—one who is a friend to her husband (Titus 2:4).
D. Have a gentle and quiet spirit to your husband (1 Peter 3:4).
E. Be available for your husband sexually as often as he desires (1 Corinthians 7:3-5).

V. Expressions of love that can be expressed by both to each other

A. Sincere apologies (Matthew 5:23-24, Romans 12:18)
B. Praising others (Proverbs 27:2, 31:28-29)
C. Listening and talking to them (James 1:19, Proverbs 18:2, 13)
D. Sharing where you hurt (2 Corinthians 6:11-13, 7:2-3)
E. Spending time with one another (2 Corinthians 12:15, 1 Thessalonians 2:8)
F. Gentle correction (Proverbs 27:6a, 1 Thessalonians 5:14)
G. Self-sacrifice (1 Corinthians 13:5, Philippians 2:3-4)
H. Submission to God-ordained authority (Ephesians 5:22-6:9, Romans 13:1-7)
I. Saying "I love you" (John 13:34)
J. Giving encouragement (1 Thessalonians 5:11, 14, Proverbs 12:25)
K. Showing appreciation (Philippians 4:14)
L. Helping each other (Acts 20:35, 1 Thessalonians 5:14)
M. Comforting each other (Romans 12:15, 2 Corinthians 1:3-4)
N. Bearing one another's burden (Galatians 6:2)
O. Warm smile or appropriate touch (Proverbs 15:30, Mark 10:13-14)
P. Phoning or writing expressions of love (3 John 1:13-14)
Q. Asking for help (Philippians 4:17)
R. Expressing forgiveness when someone has apologized (2 Corinthians 2:7, Ephesians 4:32)

(This portion adapted from Rich Thomson's The Heart of Man and The Mental Disorders)

MARRIAGE AND FAMILY

(Section Three)

YOU WANT ME TO DO WHAT? (SEX AND MARRIAGE)

I. The Purpose for Sex

    A. God designed sex for procreation (Genesis 1:28).

    B. God designed sex to be a pleasurable experience between husband and wife alone (Psalm of Solomon 4:1-51, Hebrews 13:4).

    C. God designed sex as an avenue for husband and wife to become one (Genesis 2:24-25).

    D. Sexual intimacy promotes unity, togetherness, and companionship in a pleasurable way. It allows for natural desires to be satisfied in a legitimate way.

II. The Pitfall of Unlawful Sex

    A. God will judge all who have sex outside of marriage and use people as objects to gratify their lust for pleasure and excitement (1 Thessalonians 4:4-6).

    B. Those who choose to have sex outside of marriage will bring destruction on themselves (Proverbs 5:1-23).

    C. The body is the temple of God; therefore, any sex that does not line up with God's plan is unlawful, ungodly, and will defile your body (1 Corinthians 6:12-20).

    D. If you are walking in sexual sin, you are not fulfilling the will of God, which is your sanctification (1 Thessalonians 4:3-8).

III. The Process of Repenting of Unlawful Sex

A. You must identify and confess all unlawful sex you have been participating in (Psalm 32:1-5).
B. You must seek forgiveness from those persons you have been practicing sexual sin with (James 5:16).
C. Make no more provisions for unlawful sexual activities (Romans 13:11-14). Turn away from movies, media, music, people, places, or things that have in the past lead you into sexual sin.
D. Focus on serving God and others instead of using God and others (Titus 3:14).

IV. The Practice of Sex in Marriage

A. 1 Corinthians 7:1-5 tells us that there has to be a commitment to fulfilling the sexual desires of your spouse. Sex is not to be used as a tool to manipulate or to negotiate. Sex is to be given to your spouse out of a commitment to the relationship.
B. Fulfillment of these sexual desires is to be equal in reciprocal. That means each person is to do all he or she can within the boundaries of marriage and God's will to satisfy the sexual desires of his or her spouse.
C. Sex needs to be regular and continuous. Celibacy in marriage is not what God intended. Single people are to be celibate, and married people are to have sex.
D. You must accept that your body is no longer your own in the area of sex. You must yield your body to your spouse for his or her pleasure and he or she must yield their body to you for your pleasure.

HOW TO AFFAIR PROOF YOUR MARRIAGE

I. The Myths about Marriage

A. Marriage was designed to make you happy (Proverbs 14:12)
B. Marriage will compensate for your past failures (Proverbs 14:12)
C. Marriage will fulfill all my desires (Proverbs 14:12)

II. Why Do Partners Cheat?

A. Partners cheat because their mind is set on the natural inclinations of their heart instead yielding to the power of the Holy Spirit (Mark 7:17-23).
B. Partners cheat because they are walking by their flesh (Galatians 5:16-21).
C. Partners cheat because they are self-serving instead self-sacrificing (2 Timothy 3:1-5).

III. Five major dynamics that build a relationship

A. Time – allowing yourself moments to get to know the other person
B. Talking – sharing and discussing various ideas and topics
C. Transparency – exposing emotions, desires, affections, concerns, or pains
D. Trust – developing a confidence in or a sense of security in a person
E. Touching – allowing another to caress you in intimate ways
(Insight adapted from Dr. Ivory Varner)

IV. The Anatomy of Affair

A. Emotional readiness/Unchecked thoughts
B. Growing awareness of a particular person
C. Time spent thinking about the attractiveness of the other person
D. Innocent meeting
E. Time spent comparing the other person with present mate
F. Time spent thinking about the negative, unpleasant aspect of his or her present situation; unhappy and unfulfilled in preset situation
G. Engineering circumstances so it appears unintentional
H. Public lingering
I. Private lingering
J. Time spent dwelling on how good the other person makes him or her feel
K. More frequent meeting for apparently legitimate purposes
L. Pleasurable isolation
M. Affectionate embracing
N. Denial, rationalization, justification

O. Passionate embracing

P. Sexual encounter

Q. Deviousness, deceitfulness, covert meetings

R. Struggle with conscience, vacillation (guilt, blame-shifting, etc)

S. Living double life, keeping up appearances

T. Mate, or other significant person finds out and he or she is confronted.

U. Initially, they may deny it and condemn the other person for being suspicious.

V. Eventually, if he or she continues in the affair, he or she is forced to admit what is happening at which point he or she either:

1. Decides to continue, yet remain married to present mates for the sake of children, etc.

2. Decides to repent and seek help

3. Decides to divorce present mate thinking that it will bring him or her the happiness

(Insight Adapted from Wayne Mack)

V. 16 key principles that may help you to affair proof your marriage

A. Develop a close relationship with Jesus Christ.

B. Take every thought captive to the obedience of Christ.

C. Focus on fulfilling your role as Husband/Wife not what you are not getting from your husband/wife.

D. Develop a time of prayer, devotion, and Bible Study you can do together.

E. Don't compare your mate to others.

F. Don't do for others what you are unwilling to do for your spouse.

G. Don't allow another man or woman to do for you what your spouse is responsible for doing for you.

H. Avoid conversation and physical contact with others that carry sexual over-tones.

I. Avoid magazines and entertainment that glorifies sex outside of marriage.

J. Avoid developing friendships with the opposite sex that do not include your spouse.

K. Set boundaries on the time, talking and transparency you spend with co-workers, employees, neighbors and associates of the opposite sex.

L. Stop demanding that your spouse make you happy.

M. Stay away from anyone or anything that would lead you to sin against your spouse (Hebrews 13:4).

N. Develop thoughtful ways to give love to and spend time with your spouse (Romans 12:9-13).

O. Identify burdens and needs of spouse and seek to meet them.

P. Ask for what you want without holding back what your spouse's needs.

Marriage and Family

(Section Four)

Developing Effective Communication in Marriage

Definition of Communication: the transferring and receiving of information so that one may understand and respond in the proper way to the information.

I. **Before we develop in effective communication we must understand why communication was _created_.**

    A. Communication was created so that we may understand and respond properly to the **_Person of God_** (John 1:1-18).

    B. Communication was created so that we may understand and respond properly to the **_creation of God_** (Genesis 1: 1-31, Psalm 19:1-6).

    C. Communication was created so that we may understand and respond properly to the **_commands of God_** (Psalm 119:34, 73, 144).

    D. Communication was created so that we may understand and respond properly to **_one another_** (Ephesians 4:29).

II. **Effective communication is tied to understanding the _commonness_ of communication (Insight from Creating Understanding by Donald K. Smith)**

    A. Communication comes from the root word **_communis_**- the common and public connections shared by people.

    B. Communication was not intended to be reduced to just **_transmitting of facts_**.

    C. Communication was meant to be an involvement of people on a common and public level in the sharing of information to the building of **_commonness of understanding_**.

    D. Tools transmit facts, **_people_** get involved.

III. Effective communication is tied to understanding the *control* of communication.

A. Communication *reflects* what's in our **_hearts_** (Luke 6:44-45).
B. Communication *defines*, and *interprets* our **_perspective_** of life (Luke 6:44-45).
C. Communication *exposes* the system of life by which we **_operate_** (1 John 4:5-6).
D. Communication *directs* and *shapes* our **_relationships_** with others (Proverbs 12:18).

IV. The *carelessness* of listening to your spouse according to your own understanding leads to foolishness. (Proverbs 3:5, 28:26)

A. When you listen to your spouse according to your own understanding, you tend to interpret the conversation by your **_picture_** of them, allowing your opinions to determine how you listen, leading to foolishness.
B. When you listen to your spouse according to your own understanding, you tend to interpret the conversation according to your **_preferences_**, allowing what you want them to door think in relation to the matter to determine how you listen, leading to foolishness.
C. When you listen to others according to your spouse, according to your own understanding, you tend to interpret the conversation according to your **_pain_**, allowing your disappointments, hurts, and frustrations to determine how you listen, leading to foolishness.
D. When you listen to your spouse according to your own understanding, you tend to interpret the conversation according to your **_passion_**, allowing what you want from them to determine how you listen, leading to foolishness.

V. The _carefulness_ of listening to your spouse according to God's Wisdom leads discernment. (Proverbs 8:32-35)

    A. When you listen to your spouse according to God's wisdom you can seek determine if the issue is a _**matter of preference-**_ neither right or wrong; no moral implication; just the way your spouse prefers something to happen or to be.

    B. When you listen to your spouse according to God's wisdom you can seek to determine if the issue is a _**matter of conscience-**_ neither right or wrong but is held as a conviction by your spouse as right or wrong according to their personal acquired standard.

    C. When you listen to spouse according to God's wisdom you can seek to determine if the issue is a _**matter of wisdom-**_ seeking to determine was good, better, best course of action in a situation.

    D. When you listen to your spouse according to God's wisdom you can seek to determine if the issue is a _**matter of sin-**_ a moral situation whereby your spouse is either doing what God has commanded or is disobeying what God has commanded.
    (Concepts A-D adapted from Dr. Stuart Scott)

VI. You must be _cautious_ to listen to your spouse with the intent to gain knowledge about them. (Proverbs 18:15)

    A. You should make sure you have correctly _**heard**_ your spouse's words.

    B. You should seek to understand what your spouse _**means**_ by their words.

    C. You should seek to understand what your spouse is _**feeling**_ through their words.

    D. You should seek to understand what your spouse is trying to _**accomplish**_ through their words.
    (Concepts A-D adapted from the _War of Words_ by Paul Tripp)

VII. You must _consider_ what needs to be said in the context of a situation in order to communicate according to God's purpose to your spouse. (Proverbs 15:28)

    A. When you are pondering how to answer you must consider the _**person**_ with whom you are speaking. You should ask yourself: "What do I know about this person that should shape what I am about so say?"

B. When you are pondering how to answer you must consider the ***problem.*** You should ask yourself: "What is the real need or problem and how should I address it?"

C. When you are pondering how to answer you must consider the ***process*** by which you are going to communicate. You should ask yourself: "Is this way I'm about to go about this beneficial to this person?"

D. When pondering how to answer you must consider the ***precepts*** of God's Word. You should ask yourself: "What does God's Word have to say about this?"

(Concepts A-D adapted from the ***War of Words*** by Paul Tripp)

VIII. You must be ***committed*** to honesty in your conversation with your spouse. (Ephesians 4:25)

A. You should seek to be ***honest*** in your communication with your spouse.

B. You should speak up or speak out with the truth having your spouse's ***welfare*** in mind.

C. You should speak up or speak out after you have dealt with your own ***motives*** and sin issues.

D. The only time you should be silent in a matter is when you realize that you are not going to ***build up*** your spouse.

IX. The words you ***choose*** to communicate to your spouse must be a benefit to them Ephesians 4:29)

A. The words that are spoken to your spouse should not be ***unwholesome-*** words that tear down or bypasses the issues and tunes in on your spouse's character to be critical instead of caring.

B. The words that are spoken to your spouse should be ***edifying***- words that build up your spouse and tunes in on the real issues; words that build bridges to godly connecting and spiritual growth.

C. The words that are spoken to your spouse should not be ***unnecessary*** or useless words that are for the advancement of the speaker's personal agenda. The words that are spoken should be words that are needed, ***necessary*** or useful for the moment to benefit your spouse.

D. The words that are spoken to your spouse should not render accusations but ***minister grace***- words that are kind, helpful and show goodwill regardless of what is being shared (sin matters, preference matters, wisdom matters, conscience matters).

X. *Lies* **in communication represent the character of Satan leading one to use communication apart from the design for which God created and can lead to the downfall of your spouse. (Proverbs 14: 5, 25)**

    A. You can bring harm to your spouse by communicating ***misinformation***- speaking information that is partially the truth or information that is completely wrong.

    B. You can bring harm to your spouse by communicating ***misrepresentations***- speaking information from your perception not the truth; not presenting them properly, carefully or truthfully.

    C. You can bring harm to others by communicating ***exaggerations***- speaking information about your spouse by describing it larger, better, or worse than it really is.

    D. You can bring harm to your spouse by communicating ***allegations***- making unfounded assertions about your spouse; implying something is fact without proof.
       (Concepts A-D adapted from the book Friendly Fire by Jim Morris)

XI. You must be *careful* not to talk too much knowing that the more you talk sin is inevitable. (Proverbs 10:19)

    A. Words are to be few to keep yourself from ***sinning*** in speech (Proverbs 10:19).

    B. Words are to be few to keep yourself from ***trouble*** as result of your speech (Proverbs 21:23).

    C. Words are to be few to keep yourself from ***quarrelling*** in your speech (Proverbs 17:14).

    D. Words are to be few that you may be able to ***listen*** more (James 1:19).

Marriage and Family

(Section Five)

Why can't we all just get along in our marriages?
James 4:1-10

Definition of Conflict: State of war, individual disputes or battles between people which manifest itself in attitudes, words and actions

I. Issues that lead to conflict

    A. Conflicting Personal Preferences (Acts 15:36-41)
    B. Preoccupation with personal agendas (Acts 16: 16-22)
    C. Sinful Attitudes and Actions (James 3:13-16)
    D. Unmet needs (Acts 6:1)

II. Selfish Reason we Confront each other and Produce Conflict (James 3:13-16)

    A. Trying to arrange for our opinions to be agreed with or our preferences to be realized so we confront leading to conflict
    B. Presuming to know the other person's motives and actions leading to confrontation producing conflict
    C. Pointing things out in others that irritate and anger us that we want them to confess and change for our comfort and benefit instead of leading people to see sin that God wants them to confess and change for His Glory and their benefit
    D. Using scripture to attack others instead of using it to help others see their sin and confess and repent unto God

III. The root cause of conflict can be traced back to desires you have turned into lusts and are demanding others to satisfy (James 4:1-3)

    A. Desires from within wage war against our mind, will, and affections

    B. Here are some examples theses desires:

        1. To be in control—to regulate what people say, think, and do according to   your ideals or preferences
        2. To be loved by others—to have others seek your highest good at all times
        3. To be accepted by others—to be approved of
        4. To be understood by others—to have others comprehend you accordingly
        5. To never be hurt or disappointed by others—to always have people meet your expectations
        6. To be respected by others—to be treated with reverence
        7. To be served by others—to have your needs met
        8. To have personal preferences accommodated at all times—to have others to do things your way all the time
        9. To be viewed as competent by others—to have others see you as intelligent
        10. To be approved of by others—to be well received by others
        11. To belong to someone—to be in union with another
        12. To be held in high regard by others—to be seen as somebody in the eyes of others
        13. To be significant to others—to be valuable to others
        14. To be satisfied by others—to receive pleasure accordingly
        15. To maintain a favorable position with others—to never lose ground with others
        16. To be secure—to be safe with others
        17. To never be alone—to always have someone in your life

    C. Your appetite for these desires leads you to be overly preoccupied with satisfying these desires resulting in all types of conflict.

    D. Your appetite for these desires leads you to sin to satisfy these desires and to sin when these desires are not satisfied resulting in all types of conflict and self -serving prayers.

IV. Four Key Things God may be trying to Show you in your Conflict (James 4:4-6)

    A. Consider **_desires_** that have preoccupied your mind, will, emotions, and affections in ungodly ways leading you to be friendly with the world and compromise your fellowship with God.

    B. Consider your **_ungodly ways_** of thinking, speaking, and behaving in pursuit of your lustful desires leading you to be friendly with the world and compromise your fellowship with God.

    C. Consider the **_people you are using or hurting_** to satisfy your lustful desires leading you to be friendly with the world and compromise your fellowship with God.

    D. Consider the **_areas of your life where you refuse to obey God_** leading you to be friendly with the world and compromise your fellowship with God.

The Four "P" s to look for when there is Conflict

Perception – Pay attention to conversations whereby you tend to discuss matters and concerns from your limited interpretation alone; making yourselves the hero, or the victim

Proverbs 14:12 – There is a way which seems right to a man, but its end is the way of death

---

Pain – Pay attention to conversations whereby you tend to talk more about how you have been disappointed or let down by others above how you have let down and disappointed others

Proverbs 13:12 – Hope deferred makes the heart sick, but desired fulfilled is a tree of life

Preference – Pay attention to areas in your life whereby you are more concerned with your way of things being done above loving others

Romans 14:16 – Therefore do not let what is for you a good thing be spoken of as evil

---

Passion – Pay attention to conversations whereby you are grumbling, complaining, or angry as a result of not getting what you want or getting what you don't want from others; exposing how you treasure getting your way above loving God's way

James 3:16 – For where jealousy and selfish ambition exist, there is disorder and every evil thing

V. Four Key Steps to Resolving Conflict (James 4:7-10)

A. First, examine yourself to see where you have sinned in the conflict. Ask yourself:
1. Were my words seasoned with grace or sin?
2. Was I grumbling, complaining, slandering, or gossiping?
3. Were my words negative, critical, hurtful or destructive?
4. Have I exaggerated the truth?
5. Did I handle my responsibilities in the matter?
6. Did I keep my word in the matter?
7. Did I respect or rebel against God-given authority?
8. Would I want someone to treat me the way I treated this person?
9. What desire was I preoccupied with and what did I do to satisfy it?
10. Did I withhold love?

B. Second, confess your sins to God and to the person with whom you've had the conflict and begin to alter your attitude and actions in the area you have confessed. The process would be as follows:
1. Talk with God about your specific sin and renounce it immediately.
2. Admit to others how you have specifically sinned against them in attitude and /or action.
3. Ask their forgiveness of your sin against them.
4. Accept the consequences of your sin and make the necessary restitution.
5. Alter your attitudes, actions, and relationship patterns to line up with the standards of God.
(Adopted from Peacemakers Ministries from Ken Sande)

C. Third, at the appropriate time, address the sin issue of the other with whom you had the conflict with the intent to restore them, and resolve t the matter and not with the intent to destroy them. You would do this by:

1. Speaking the truth in love
2. Helping him or her work through their faults accordingly
3. Allowing him or her time to respond
4. Resting and waiting on God to do His Will
5. Being at peace with the person or persons involved
6. Covering it and moving on when the issue is resolved

D. Fourth, if the issue remains unsettled, you want to get others involved to resolve the issue without taking sides in the issue.

The Two "P"s to Practice in Resolving Conflict

Precept - Interpret the situation from a biblical perspective with specific principles from the Bible that govern the problems accordingly

Proverbs 3:5-6 - Trust in the LORD with all your heart and do not lean on your own understanding. In all your ways acknowledge Him, and He will make your paths straight.

Practice - Identify specific ways to think, communicate, behave, relate, and serve that will help you put off the sin problem and put on the right way of living

James 1:22-25 - But prove yourselves doers of the word, and not merely hearers who delude themselves. For if anyone is a hearer of the word and not a doer, he is like a man who looks at his natural face in a mirror; for once her has looked at himself and gone away, he has immediately forgotten what kind of person he was. But one who looks intently at the perfect law, the law of liberty, and abides by it, not having become a forgetful hearer but an effectual doer, this man will be blessed in what he does.

MARRIAGE AND FAMILY

(Section Six)

The Problem of Worshiping our Spouses Above Worshiping God
(Romans 1:18-25)

I. We tend to see our spouses as avenues to satisfy our desires/cravings.

    A. Our spouses become an avenue to bring satisfaction to us.

    B. They become objects we use instead of people we love.

    C. They have to perform for us in order to provide all that we deem important from them which means they cannot fail us or disappoint us.

II. We tend to focus on having our way with our spouse instead of loving God's way.

    A. Having our way without our spouse becomes more important that loving them.

    B. We become consumed with how to get our spouses to do what we want.

    C. We make them the source and the solution to our problems and satisfaction.

III. We tend to live for what we want from our spouse instead of living for God.

    A. We believe that what we want from our spouses cannot be lived without

    B. We start to elevate our desires to needs.

    C. As we elevate our desires to needs, they become demands on our spouses that cannot be denied without negative consequences to them from us.

IV. We overcome worshiping our spouses by:

    A. Confessing and repenting of making our spouses and the outcome of events idols and lust of our Hearts (Ezekiel 14:1-11) (See the book ***With All Your Heart*** by Nicolas Ellen)

    B. Studying, learning and accepting the sovereignty of God in all things (Ecclesiastes 3:1-11, 7:13-14, 9:1, 11:5, Colossians 1:15-17)

    C. Accepting that fact that every good and perfect gift is from God not our spouses (James 1:16-17)

D. Accepting the fact all that we need comes from God not our spouse (2Peter 1:1-3, Philippians 4:19, Romans 8:31-32, Psalm 145:8-16, Hebrews 4:16)

E. Seeking to help our spouses live a life to please God; instead trying to manipulate them into a life pleasing us (Galatians 1:10, 1Corinthains 10:31)

F. Serving our spouses according to God's Will and not according to how we feel or what we want from them in return (1Corinthians 13:1-8, Romans 12:9-21, John 13:34-35, Luke 6:31-38)

G. Setting our minds on God's agenda in every aspect of our lives and seeking to live according to that agenda (Matthew 6:33, Colossians 3:1-25, Ephesians 5:1-18)

V. We must allow these five key perspectives to become the things we consider when relating to our spouses

A. We must embrace and Worship God as the Creator instead of worshiping His creation.

B. We must have a sober assessment of ourselves; seeing ourselves as Children of God being transformed into the image of Jesus Christ.

C. We must see our spouses as Children of God being transformed into the image of Jesus Christ.

D. We must value Christ above what we want from our spouses or what we want to see in our spouses' character.

E. We must stop trying to fix our spouses to satisfy our personal preferences.

MARRIAGE AND FAMILY

(Section Seven)

The Role of Fathers/Mothers/ Child

I. Fathers are not to provoke their children but to raise them to be godly (Colossians 3:21, Ephesians 6:4).

    A. Meaning – not nagging or agitating your children, but correcting, instructing, and directing children in the way of truth in all aspects of life (Ephesians 6:4)

    B. Member – to your children/children for whom you are guardian (Ephesians 6:4)

    C. Manner – as God disciplines his Children (Hebrews 12:5-11)

    D. Motive – so that your children do not lose heart, live in anger, live foolishly (Ephesians 6:4)

    E. Model – as God disciplines his Children (Hebrews 12:5-11)

    F. Magnitude – in all aspects of life (Deuteronomy 6:4-10)

    G. Manifestation – teaching their children how to live life according to God's design, disciplining their children according to the need of the moment, spending time influencing and shaping the thoughts, words, deeds, of their children to reflect the character of God (Ephesians 6:4)

II. Mothers are to love their Children (Titus 2:4).

    A. Meaning – to cultivate a friendship love with them (Titus 2:4)

    B. Member – to your children for whom you are guardian (Titus 2:4)

    C. Manner – as Jesus would cultivate a friendship with us (John 15:14-15)

    D. Motive – so that your children may grow up to be godly children (Proverbs 22:6)

    E. Model – as Christ so loved His Disciples (John 15:12-14)

    F. Magnitude – to the extent that it assists the father to keep children under loving control in the discipline and instruction of the Lord (Proverbs 14:1, 31:26-28)

    G. Manifestation - teaching their children how to live life according to God's design, disciplining their children according to the need of the moment, spending time influencing and shaping the thoughts, words, deeds, of their children to reflect the character of God (Proverbs 14:1, 31:26-28, Psalm 128:1-3)

III. Children are to obey their parents (Colossians 3:20, Ephesians 6:1)

A. Meaning - to follow the instructions and guidelines of parents in all aspects of life as long as it does not violate God's Standards (Ephesians 6:1)

B. Member – to your parents/guardians (Ephesians 6:1)

C. Manner – as Christ submitted to the Headship of God the Father; as if you were submitting the Lord Himself(Philippians 2:5-8)

D. Motive – to be well pleasing to the Lord that it may be well with you; that you may live long on earth (Ephesians 6:1-2)

E. Model – as Christ submitted to the Headship of God the Father (Philippians 2:5-8)

F. Magnitude – in everything (Ephesians 6:1-2)

G. Manifestation – not neglecting the instructions given by parents, showing respect to parents in words and actions when you are with them and when you are away from them, living a life that displays God's character and brings honor not shame to parents (Ephesians 6:1-2)

Foundations for Child Rearing
(Information adapted from *Shepherding a Child's Heart* by: Tedd Tripp)

A. Parents are to exercise their authority as God's agent. They are to direct their children to the glory of God and the benefit of the Child. They are not to direct their children according to their personal agendas or their selfish ambitions (Ephesians 6:4).

B. Parents are to shepherd the heart of their children into God's wisdom. They are to help children come to understand who they are and why they do what they do. They are to teach their children who God is, how He operates, and how they are to relate to Him (Deuteronomy 6:1-9).

C. Parents are to lead their children to the Gospel of Jesus Christ. They need to help their children understand why they need God. They are to help their children understand how and why they are slaves to sin from the inside out. They need to help them understand the power and purpose of the Gospel in relation to their lives (2Corinthians 5:20-21, Romans 3:1-31).

D. Since the heart of the child determines the behavior of a child, parents must learn the process of looking at behavior as a means to identifying what is in the heart to understand what is driving the decisions of their children (Luke 6:43-45).

E. Parents must attend to the behavior and the heart of their children to facilitate change from the inside out. They must help children understand the connection between their heart and their behavior and their need for Christ to save them from themselves. (Proverbs 20:5, Romans 3:1-31, 2Corinthians 5:20-21).

F. Parents must discipline and instruct their children. They must instruct them in what to do and why they do what they do. They must discipline and correct them when they do wrong and show them why and how they must do things God's way through a genuine relationship with Jesus Christ (Ephesians 6:4).

G. Parents must help children understand that they are living a life either in rebellion or submission to Christ (Galatians 6:7-8).

H. Parents must help children understand that true life and satisfaction will only come through a right relationship with Christ and nothing else (John 6:26-71).

I. Parents must evaluate their own life before God to see where they stand and how their walk with God is influencing the life of their children (2Corinthians 13:5).

MARRIAGE AND FAMILY

(Section Eight)

The Shaping Influences With Children
(Information adapted from *Shepherding a Child's Heart* by Tedd Tripp)

(Galatians 6:7-8, Ephesians 6:1-4, Luke 6:43-45, Romans 8:1-15, Ezekiel 18:1-32)

A. Shaping influences are those events and circumstances in a child's developmental years that impact who the person is today.

B. The condition of a child's life is determined by his response to shaping influences.

C. Parents either see shaping influences as the determining factor that will determine the outcome of their children or they deny that the shaping influences impact the outcome of their children at all.

D. Shaping influences are important but your son or daughter responds to shaping influences according to their perspective of God and relationship or lack thereof they have with of God.

E. If they have a right relationship with God they will respond to shaping influences in a manner that will be God-honoring and beneficial to them. If they do not have a right relationship with God, they will rebel against even against the best shaping influence you can provide.

F. Children become who they are as they respond to your parenting and shaping influences either out of a heart that seeks to please God or out of a heart that seeks to please self; therefore, children are not passive receivers to shaping influences; they are active responders according to the orientation of their hearts.

G. Since shaping influences have a major impact on the person your child becomes we must examine a few of them for you to consider with your children:

1. ***Structure of Family Life*** – Is it a family with a Mother and Father? How many parents is the child exposed to? Are there stepparents involved? Is it a family of two generations or three? Are both parents alive and functioning in the home? How are the parenting roles structured? Are there other children or is the family life organized around only one child? What is the birth order of the Children? How close or distant are they in terms of age, ability, interest, or personality? How does the child's personality blend with other members of the family?

2. ***Family Values*** – What is important to the parents? What is worth a fuss and what passes without notice? Are people more important than things? Do parents get more stressed over a hole in the school pants or a fight between schoolmates? What philosophies and ideas has the child heard? Are children to be seen and not heard in this home? What are the spoken and unspoken rules of the family? Where does God fit into the family? Is life organized around knowing and loving God or is the family on a different level? Are the values in the home based on human tradition and the basic principles of this world or on Christ? Where are the secrets kept and where are they told? Are the relationship with neighbors instinctively open or closed? (Colossians 2:8-23)

3. ***Family Roles*** – What is the role of the father? What is the role of the mother? What is the role of the children? Does dad do everything, something, or nothing in the house? Does mom do everything, something, or nothing in the house? Are children the maidservants of the home? Are Children the King and Queen of the home? How does stuff get done? Who pays the bills? Who arranges for appointments? (Colossians 3:18-25)

4. ***Family Conflict Resolution*** – Does the family know how to resolve or talk about its problems? Do family members resolve things or do they simply walk away? Are problems solved by biblical principles or by power? (James 3:13-4:10)

5. ***Family Response to Failure*** – How are failures treated? Are children made to feel Foolish? Are they mocked for their failures? Does the family find amusement at the expense of family members? Do they neutralize the effects of failure? Do family members encourage others or discourage others when they fail?(Ecclesiastes 4:9-12)

6. ***Family History-*** Is there divorce in the family? Is it a blended family situation? Have there been many deaths in the family? Has there been many health problems in the family? Has there been any money problem in the family? Has the family moved around a lot?

7. **<u>Political Views</u>** – What has been the politics of your family? How has that influenced the mindset of the family? Are there democrats or republicans in the family? Are these views developed or forced upon the children? Are children taught to respect or disrespect the president according to his political party? (Romans 13:1-7)
8. **<u>*Ethnic Views*</u>** – How does your family view various races and ethnic groups? Do they see one as superior to another? Are they taught to get along with all? Are they taught not to associate with particulars? Are friends diverse or of the same race? (Luke 6:31-38)

MARRIAGE AND FAMILY

(Section Nine)

God Orientation and Child Development
(Information adapted from *Shepherding a Child's Heart* by: Tedd Tripp)

A. A child's orientation towards God will determine how he develops and the direction of his life (Galatians 5:16-24, Galatians 6:7-8).

B. The Bible teaches that man sins because he is a sinner. Children are not an exception. Children are not morally neutral. They come from the womb wayward and sinful (Psalm 58:3, Psalm 51:5).

C. Children either respond to God by faith or they suppress the truth in unrighteousness (Psalm 58:3).

D. "Folly is bound up in the heart of a child, but the rod of discipline will drive it far from him" (Proverbs 22:15).

E. Children are not the sum total of what you put in them. They interact with life either out of a true faith in Christ or with a life of unbelief in Christ (Romans 8:5-14).

F. As you are parenting children, you must distinguish between immaturity and sin against God. They are not the same.

G. Immaturity is when one is speaking or acting in a way that shows a lack of development in a particular area which may result in clumsiness or inconsistency (1Corinthains 13:11, Hebrews 5:11-14).

H. Sin is when one thinks, speaks, or acts in ways that are a violation of God's will and ways (1John 3:4-10).

I. One can grow out of immaturity. One must confess and repent out of sin and turn to God to cleanse, and deliver him from it (1John 1:9, Proverbs 28:13-14, Hebrews 5:11-14).

J. You will have a hard time helping your children develop unless you see your children's behavior as a reflection of a heart that is either oriented towards God or a heart that is oriented towards serving self (Galatians 5:16-25).

K. You must be faithful in seeking to shepherd the hearts of children in the direction of knowing and serving God, knowing you have no control over the outcome of their lives (Colossians 1:28, 2Timothy 2:24-26).

L. When children are driven by Godly principles they will become a slave to God leading to genuine righteousness and eternal life in Christ (Romans 6:21).

M. When children are driven by the flesh they will becomes slaves of sin (Proverb 5:21-23).

N. Every choice that children make is driven by thoughts rooted in pleasing self or thoughts rooted in pleasing God. Their thoughts are driven by a love of self and love of pleasure or a love of God and love of others. Their actions/reactions/feelings in circumstances exposes the nature of their heart orientation (Proverbs 23:7a, Romans 8:5-14, 2Timohty 3:1-9, 1John 2:3-11).

O. When Children have a heart oriented towards self, eight key things will begin to manifest:

1. Their minds will be set on things below instead of things above leading them to making self interest a priority over God's will (Philippians 3:17-19, James 3:13-4:3).
2. Their desires will become preoccupations resulting in using people, places, possessions, and power to satisfy these desires (Ezekiel 14:1-3).
3. They will build their lives around these desires that have become preoccupations (Philippians 3:17-19).
4. They will become servants of their flesh to satisfy these desires that have become preoccupations (Galatians 5:16-21).
5. They will become a slave to that which they pursue (2Peter 2:18-19).
6. They will develop sinful habits that are hard to break. (Proverbs 5:21-22).
7. They will reap negative consequences of their sinful habits and idolatrous lust pursuits (Galatians 6:7-8).
8. They will have a negative effect on the lives of those around them (1Corinthians 5:1-6).

P.   We must seek to be faithful to work on leading our children into a heart oriented towards God knowing that the outcome is not determined by us (1Corinthains 3:7-8).

1. We must identify desires or cravings that have preoccupied the minds of our children and seek to lead them to confess and repent of these things and turn to Jesus Christ for Salvation (Proverbs 28:13-14, John 3:16-18).
2. We must seek to help our children replace these desires or cravings that have preoccupied their minds with attitudes, words, actions, relationship patterns, and service that glorifies God (Ephesians 4:17-32, Colossians 3:1-25).
3. We must seek to help them make God a priority in all that they think, say, and do (1Corinthians 10:31).
4. Our desire is that there will be a change in their actions/reactions/ feelings resulting in a heart oriented towards God.

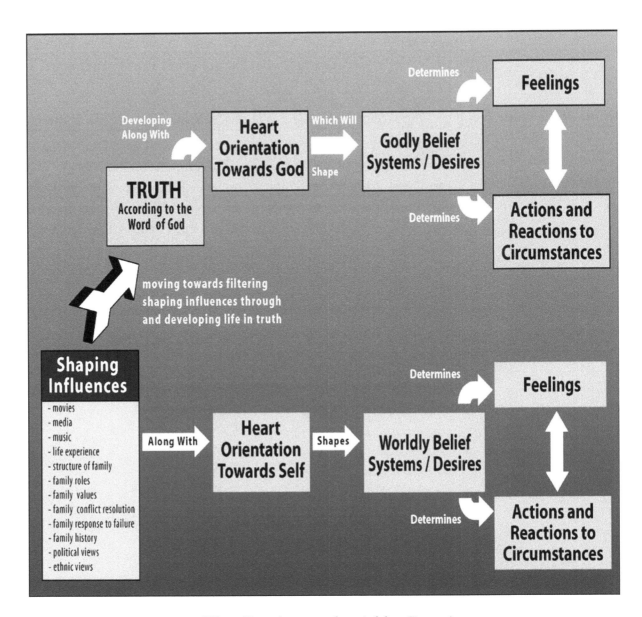

(Chart Development by: Adrian Baxter)

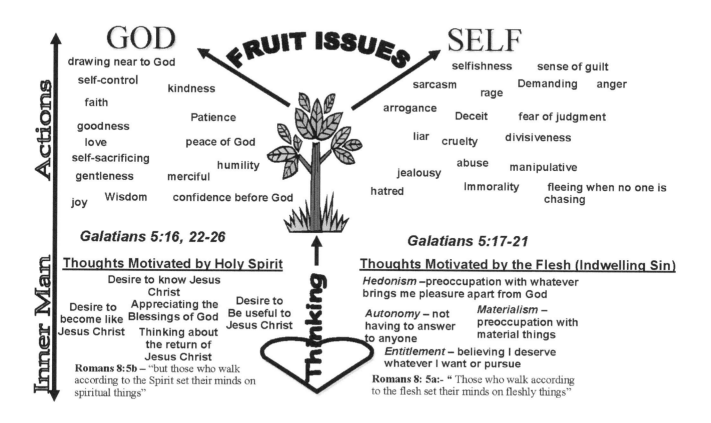

GOD

FRUIT ISSUES

SELF

Actions

drawing near to God

self-control   kindness

faith

goodness   Patience

love   peace of God

self-sacrificing

gentleness   humility

joy   Wisdom   merciful   confidence before God

Galatians 5:16, 22-26

selfishness   sense of guilt

sarcasm   rage   Demanding   anger

arrogance   Deceit   fear of judgment

liar   cruelty   divisiveness

jealousy   abuse   manipulative

hatred   Immorality   fleeing when no one is chasing

Galatians 5:17-21

Inner Man

Thinking

Thoughts Motivated by Holy Spirit

Desire to know Jesus Christ

Desire to become like Jesus Christ

Appreciating the Blessings of God

Thinking about the return of Jesus Christ

Desire to Be useful to Jesus Christ

Romans 8:5b – "but those who walk according to the Spirit set their minds on spiritual things"

Thoughts Motivated by the Flesh (Indwelling Sin)

Hedonism –preoccupation with whatever brings me pleasure apart from God

Autonomy – not having to answer to anyone

Materialism – preoccupation with material things

Entitlement – believing I deserve whatever I want or pursue

Romans 8: 5a:- " Those who walk according to the flesh set their minds on fleshly things"

Graphics by Cathy Poulos

Review the Situation?

AMBITION

My goal in life is to please God. (2 Corinthians 5:9)

I please God by being like Jesus Christ. (Ephesians 4:11-15)

God knows I will not be perfect, but He does expect me to be growing. (Ephesians 4:22-24)

(Adapted from Mark Dutton)

2 Help children identify their self-centered thoughts, feelings, words, behavior, and relationship patterns in the situation.

9 Help Children replace and display thoughts, feelings, words, behavior, and relationship patterns that are God-Centered in this situation.

Thinking

7 Help Children identify the God-centered motives needed to replace the self-centered motives in this situation. 1Timothy 1:5

6 Help Children identify the God-centered thoughts needed to replace the self-centered thoughts in this situation.

3 Help Children identify their self-centered thoughts in the situation.

4 Help Children identify their self-centered motives in the situation.

8 Help Children identify the God-centered desires needed to replace the self-centered desires in this situation.

5 Help Children identify their self-centered desires in the situation.

God-Centered

Self-Centered

Walk in the Spirit

Recognize Repent and Replace

Luke 9:23-25

1 John 1:9
Ephesians 4:17-24;
Philippians 2:5

Adapted from curriculum presented in BC590s: Counseling Practicum, Dr. John Street professor, The Master's College, Santa Clarita, CA July 2004. Graphics by Cathy Poulos

Marriage and Family

(Section Ten)

Embracing Biblical Methods for Childrearing
(Information adapted from *Shepherding a Child's Heart* by Tedd Tripp)

I. *Communication (A Key Method for Childrearing)*

A. Communication is to be used to not only teach children how to listen but to also teach them how to share their thoughts (Proverbs 20:5).

B. We must use communication as an opportunity to connect with our children so that we can evaluate what is happening in their hearts (Proverbs 20:5).

C. We need to learn to listen to them in such a way that will help us to see things from their perspective in order to provide them with God's insights according to their need at the moment (Proverbs 18:13, Ephesians 4:29).

D. Communication is to be used to help children understand, express and deal with themselves (Proverbs 20:5).

E. Communication is to be used to help children understand the way and will of God and what that means for their lives (Proverbs 4:1-27).

F. Communication is to be used to help children learn how to deal with the temptations that will show up in their lives (Proverbs 5:1-14).

G. Overall we should seek to use communication to lead our children into salvation and to lead our children into sanctification (maturity in Christ) knowing the outcome is not determined by us (2Timothy 2:24-26).

H. We may use words of:
   1. *Encouragement*– to provide inspiration and hope (1Thessalonians 5:11)
   2. *Correction* – to give your children insight as to what is wrong and what may be done to correct the problem. (Proverbs 12:1)
   3. *Rebuke* – to acknowledge disapproval at wrong behavior (Proverbs 19:25)
   4. *Entreaty* – to urge a child to walk in the paths of wisdom and faith (Proverbs 4:10-19)
   5. *Instruction*- to provide a lesson, a precept, or information that will help our children to understand their world, themselves, God and others according to God's perspective and within a framework they can grasp (Ephesians 6:4)
   6. *Warning* – to provide awareness to the consequences of bad choices (Hebrews 12:15-17, 25)

II. *The Rod (A Key Method for Childrearing)*

A. Children are born sinners (Psalm 58:3).

B. Children have a defiled heart filled with foolishness and folly (Mark 7:17-23, Proverbs 22:15).

C. If the foolish and folly goes unchecked there will be consistent foolishness and folly expressed in their behavior leading to the destruction of the child (Proverbs 13:15).

D. The folly that is in a child's heart must be driven out (Proverbs 22:15).

E. God tells us in His Word that the rod of correction is the means by which the folly is driven out (Proverbs 22:15).

F. God has not explained how the rod of correction removes folly. Therefore, we must trust God on the basis of what He said (Proverbs 3:5-8).

G. The Bible is very clear about the rod of correction:
   1. Proverbs 13:24
   2. Proverbs 22:15
   3. Proverbs 23:13-14
   4. Proverbs 29:15

H. In our use of the rod of correction, we must make a distinction between behavior that is childish and behavior that is defiant. The rod is to be used for defiant (sinful) behavior not childish silly behavior (Kids will be silly). In our use of the rod we must never discipline kids while we are in sinful anger James 1:19-20).

I. The goal of our discipline must be out of love for God and out love for our children resulting restoration not retribution (Proverbs 13:24, Hebrews 12:5-11).

J. When we use the rod as God designed it:
   1. *Show God's Authority over Mom and Dad* – as parents use the rod as God instructed, they show that they are following authority as they are working with their children to do the same (Luke 6:40).
   2. *Trains Children to be under authority* – kids must learn that everyone is under authority and that it is far better to be submissive to authority than to be against authority (Proverbs 29:15, Romans 13:1-7).
   3. *Demonstrates parental love and commitment*– proper discipline demonstrates parents are seeking to do what is best even if it bring pain (Proverbs 13:24).

   4. **May** *Yield a harvest of peace and righteousness* – properly administered discipline, while unpleasant and painful at the time, tends to yield disciplined, self controlled children (Hebrews 12:11, Proverbs 29:17).

Key Point:

Communication and the Rod are designed to work together. Rich communication will help in providing an avenue for your children to be known and understood. The rod helps to instill the value of staying within the boundaries subscribed by God (Proverbs 29:15)

Marriage and Family

(Section Eleven)

Training Objectives for Child Rearing
(Information adapted from *Shepherding a Child's Heart* by Tedd Tripp)

I. Infancy to Childhood (0 to 5yrs) (Points derived from Tedd Tripp)

A. In the first five years, the primary training objective is to teach your children to be under the authority of God (Ephesians 6:1-3).

B. Children are to learn to obey authority without delay, debate, or discussion.

C. Discipline, words of correction, and clear directives must work hand in hand because children do not give a lot of weight to words alone at this stage of life (Provides 22:15).

D. So that we may teach children to live by principles and not by mood, parents must be consistent in discipline and correction at this stage (Proverbs 29:15).

E. Obedience must not be an option so that children may not ever think that disobedience is okay. Therefore, we must stay consistent in discipline, words of correction, and clear directives (Proverbs 13:24).

F. We must consider that:
   1. When your child is old enough to resist your directives, he is old enough to be disciplined.
   2. You should allow one time for them to give the excuse "But I didn't hear you."
   3. Generally, if parents are consistent with discipline, they will find quickly that the child responds and the necessity for discipline decreases.
   4. If you are too mad to discipline properly, you must seek the face of God to repent of your anger. When you have calmed down and repented, then go deal with your child properly.

5. If you are in a public place, go to a private place where you may discipline your child properly without the pressure of public observation.

6. When you are not sure what has happened then do not spank your child. That only leads to provoking your child to anger.

II. Childhood (5 yrs to 12 yrs)

A. The primary training objective between 5-12 is to build character.

B. Your child's character must be developed in areas such as dependability, honesty, kindness, consideration, helpfulness, diligence, loyalty, humility, self-control, and moral purity as well as many others (Proverbs 22:6).

C. Your child needs biblical wisdom in dealing with issues of the heart as well as behavior (Proverbs 4:1-13).

D. The goal at this stage is to help your child see and address issues that deal more with the ugliness in their character such as selfishness or mocking (issues of defiance are hopefully secondary issues at this stage as a result of the consistency of discipline in earlier stage of training)

E. Addressing the child's character places the emphasis on issues of the heart. It enables you to get underneath behavior and address the thoughts, motives, and purposes of the heart (Luke 6:43-45).

F. If you do not deal with character and just set rules, you will end up producing children who learn to keep the rules but are weak in character. They become people whose cups are washed and clean on the outside but filthy on the inside (Matthew 23:25-28).

G. You must develop a comprehensive way to evaluate the strengths and weaknesses of your children so that you can zero in on where and how to develop their character according to the precepts of God.

H. You must develop a comprehensive way to evaluate your child's relationship to God. You must have some perception of where he/she is spiritually:
> 1. Does your child have a relationship with God?
> 2. Is your child living in a conscious need for God?
> 3. What is the content of his relationship with God?
> 4. Is he concerned to know and love God?
> 5. Is God a source of strength, comfort, and help?
> 6. Doe he make choices that reflect knowing God?
> 7. Is he moved by God's ways and truth?
> 8. Is he alive to spiritual realities?

9. Is there any evidence that he is carrying an independent relationship with God apart from you?
10. Does he ever talk about God?
11. Is his God small or grand?
12. Does he think of God as a friend, a judge, a helper, or a taskmaster?
13. Is he living out the fullness of seeing himself in Christ or is he trying to worship and serve himself?

I. You must develop a comprehensive way to evaluate your child's relationship to himself.:

1. How does your child think about himself?
2. How well does he understand himself?
3. How aware is he of his strengths and weaknesses?
4. Does he understand his personality?
5. Is he self-conscious about the propensities of his personality?
6. Is he arrogant?
7. Is he chained by fears?
8. Is he able to extend himself to others?
9. Does he have a false dependence on others?
10. Does he feel better than others or does he feel inadequate around others?
11. Is he able to stick to a task without external props?
12. Is he able to work independently?

J. You must develop a comprehensive way to evaluate your child's relationship to others:

1. What are the relationships of your children?
2. How does he deal with disappointment in people?
3. How does he respond to being sinned against?
4. What are the areas of relational strength?
5. What are the areas of relational weaknesses?

III. Teenagers to Adulthood

A. The primary objectives at this stage of parenting is to teach your children the fear of the Lord, adherence to parental instruction, and disassociation from the wicked.

B. At this stage you are seeking to motivate young people into a sense of awe and reverence for God.

C. At this stage you are seeking to motivate young people to make choices that reflect a growing comprehension of what it means to be a God worshipper.

D. You want to teach young people how to organize their lives around the fear of God instead of the fear of man (Proverbs 29:25).

E. You want to seek to influence young people to respond to things based on Scripture in all aspects of their life.

F. According to Romans 12:2-21, 1Peter 4:10-11, Ecclesiastes 5:18-20, you want to seek to help young people to:
　　1. Develop a Christian Mind about all things (Romans 12:2).
　　2. Develop relationships that are God-honoring (Romans 12:8-21).
　　3. Discover and develop a ministry that is in accordance to their giftedness (Romans 12:3-7).
　　4. Discover a career in which they can fulfill the cultural mandate and God's command that they support themselves and share with others in need.
　　5. Establish their own home and family identity as a member of the society and a part of the Body of Christ.

MARRIAGE AND FAMILY

(Section Twelve)

What Causes A Rebellious Child?

(Information adapted from <u>The Heart of Man and The Mental Disorders</u> by Rich Thomson)

Key Point: A rebellious child is one who has a pattern and lifestyle of uninterrupted sin. It is not an act of sin but a lifestyle of sin. A rebellious child is a double responsibility issue. It is the issue of the child and the issue primarily of the father. God designed the father to have such an impact in the child's life that they cannot stay in an uninterrupted pattern and lifestyle of sin due to the father's consistent involvement, instruction, and discipline. We are not talking about a father keeping children from every act of sin, but a father having enough involvement, instruction, and discipline to keep a child from staying in a pattern and lifestyle of uninterrupted sin. However, a child has the responsibility to respond to this involvement, instruction, and discipline accordingly. It is primarily the father's responsibility to instruct and discipline a child. In those situations of death of a father, or divorce, or a never married mother, God provides grace to the single parent to function accordingly. A rebellious child is the issue of a father not keeping a child under control and a child not responding accordingly to God and the authority over him. However, a loving father (mother in the case or death or divorce, or never married) will keep a child under control in the sense of keeping them from a pattern and lifestyle of uninterrupted sin, not necessarily keeping a child from committing a sin. As the child becomes an adult and able to go on their own the parent has less authority and ability to impact the decisions and lifestyle of that child. This is beyond their control. The choices of an adult child are the responsibility of that child alone not the parents—i.e. Prodigal son *(Ephesians 6:4, Colossians 3:21, 1 Timothy 3:4-5, Ezekiel 18:1-32, Luke 15:11-32.)*

    A. It takes the child's own lack of love, and the father's lack of open love toward the child and the family to produce a rebellious child—the mother may be part of the problem or part of the solution (Luke 6:31-36, Ephesians 6:1-4, 1Timothy 3:4-5).

    B. The child's own walk in Christ will produce love and obedience to his parents not rebellion (Ephesians 6:1-3).

C. Even when the child is not walking by the Spirit, the father's own open loving walk in Christ will be the source of enough love and enough loving control (both internal and external) that the child will not be able to walk in a pattern and lifestyle of uninterrupted sin. This does not mean the child will not sin. It means the child will not be able to stay in an uninterrupted pattern of sin due to the loving control of the father (1 Timothy 3:4, Titus 1:6, Ephesians 6:4, Colossians 3:21, 1 Peter 5:3, Proverbs 22:15, Luke 6:32, Proverbs 20:30).

D. If only one child in a family is rebellious, it means that the father(mother when there is no father) is not walking in God's open love; at least to that one child. His involvement, instruction, and discipline is probably lacking with that child. He is probably practicing the same sin of that one child but not dealing with it in his own life and being overly critical about in the child's life. As a result, the child is rebelling against the parent accordingly (Matthew 7:1-5, Romans 2:1).

E. If a child or teen's peers are aiding in his rebellion, it again falls to the father (mother when there is no father) to make choices which will help the child. Some examples would be breaking off friendships firmly and lovingly, father spending more personal time with the child, (seeing that the mother's priority is the home), changing the school the child attends, or even the father changing his work hours to bring loving control to the situation in order that child will not be able to stay in an uninterrupted pattern and lifestyle of sin (Ephesians 6:4, 1 Corinthians 15:33).

F. There are some rejections to this view point:
   1. Rejections
   A. God was Adam's Father and was not responsible for his rebellion (Genesis 3).
   B. The father of the prodigal son (which is a picture of God the Father's forgiving love of mankind) saw his son rebel, but he was a good loving father (Luke 15:11-32).
   2. Responses
   A. In both cases the children were adults. In neither case was the father responsible for keeping His children under control as in 1Timothy 3:4.
   B. Both Adam and the prodigal son were independent and on their own. The prodigal son was old enough to go on his own and live independently even though he was working at his father's estate. Neither account deals with child rearing.

<h1>Expressions of Love for Parents and Children</h1>

(Information Adapted from <u>The Heart of Man and The Mental Disorders</u> by Rich Thomson)

Key Point: In order to work on dealing with a rebellious child, parents must identify ways to express love to their children, and children must work on expressing love to their parents. The Bible says that sinners love those who love them. That would suggest to us that even an unbelieving child will show some acts of love as one learns to love them accordingly. How much more would this apply to a child who is a Christian? (See Luke 6:31-36.)

I. Several Ways a Father can express love to his children
  A. Provide physical nourishment (1Timothy 5:8)
   1. Be gainfully employed in order to provide food and covering for his family.
   2. Adjust the family's standard of living to his income, rather than risking repossessions and financial difficulties.
   3. Provide reasonable medical benefits and life insurance for family.
   4. Help children understand and practice good nutrition, hygiene and safety.
   5. Stay out of debt which he cannot pay off consistently so that he will not risk being able to support his family.
   6. Provide child support for his children who do not live with him.

  B. Provide relational nurture (Ephesians 6:4)
   1. Spend time with children individually and together doing what they enjoy.
   2. Hug and kiss them on a regular basis.
   3. Have a regular talk date with your children allowing them to share any and all that is on their heart with you.
   4. Listen to your children's concerns while comforting them in their sorrow and bearing the burdens with them.
   5. Share your own hurts and joys with them to help them understand you better.
   6. Guide them with wise counsel and encouragement.

  C. Do not provoke to anger (Ephesians 6:4)
   1. For every negative you have against them, provide a positive to them.
   2. Apologize to your children when you have sinned against them instead covering it up or making excuses.
   3. Be open and honest with children, and do not lie to them.
   4. Provide clear, understandable and reasonable rules and responsibilities for children as well as clear, understandable, and reasonable repercussions and consequences that will occur for violation of those rules and responsibilities.

5. Be open to reason with your children, giving them an opportunity to explain their thoughts, words, behavior, decision, etc.
6. Support them accordingly while rebuking them loving.

D. Keep them under loving control (1Timohty 3:4)
1. Do not refuse or neglect to lovingly use the rod on the children.
2. Discipline the children firmly in love, not in anger.
3. Teach children the principle of Scripture by which their behavior is being Disciplined.
4. Use discipline as a opportunity to correct and change behavior not as a opportunity to get back at for negative behavior.
5. Praise children for good behavior with same fervor you do in disciplining them for bad behavior.
6. Be equitable and fair in the reward and discipline of children.

E. Teach them truth from God's Word by which they are to live (Ephesians 6:4)
1. Have a regular time of Bible Study with children.
2. Teach children how to apply the Truth of the Word to their lives.
3. Help children to establish a Biblical World View in Aspects of life.
4. Teach children how to study the Bible for themselves.
5. Help children learn how to make godly decisions.
6. Help children learn how to identify and use their spiritual gifts.

II. Several Ways a mother can express love to her children
A. Be a friend to children as Christ was to his disciples (Titus 2:3-4)
1. Offer loving corrective comments when they need a balanced perspective.
2. Assign and train the children to do their household chores.
3. Be at their activities and support them there.
4. See that they receive whatever medical attention the family is able to provide.
5. Train the children in homemaking skills.
6. Nurse them back to health when they are ill.

B. Assist husband in keeping children under loving control (Titus 2:3-4)
1. Expect and enforce the same standards for the children when her husband is not present as she does when he is present.
2. Send the children back to their father when they attempt to enlist her on their side against him.
3. Discipline the children firmly in love, not in anger.
4. Teach children the principle of Scripture by which their behavior is being Disciplined.
5. Use discipline as a opportunity to correct and change behavior not as a opportunity to get back at for negative behavior.
6. Communicate with the children that she is keeping their father abreast of what they are doing and not doing accordingly when he is not present.

C. Teach them truth from God's Word by which they are to live (Titus 2:3-4)
1. Have a regular time of Bible Study with children.
2. Teach children how to apply the Truth of the Word to their lives.
3. Help children to establish a Biblical World View in Aspects of life.

4. Teach children how to study the Bible for themselves .
5. Help children learn how to make godly decisions.
6. Help children learn how to identify and use their spiritual gifts.

D. Next to her husband, make taking care of the children a priority (Titus 2:3-4)
1. Seek to be at home when the children leave for school and return from school.
2. Be at home to guide children's choices of TV, video games, and other activities.
3. Supervise the planning and serving of nutritious meals, doing the dishes, doing the laundry, and the cleaning the house.
4. Be at home when kids are sick to support and nurture.
5. Take time at home to dialogue and encourage children.
6. Take time at home to play with and have fun with children.

III. Several Ways Children can express love to their parents
A. Obey parents (Ephesians 6:1).
1. Do what they are asked to do when they are asked to do it.
2. Speak to parents with respect.
3. Accept thankfully the limitations and freedoms which they have given them.
4. Follow their parents' rules when they are not present.
5. Ask their parents for permission to do things away from home and in the home where rules and understanding have not been given; don't assume it is okay; ask to see if it is okay.
6. Come home at the appointed times.

B. Honor Parents (Ephesians 6:2-3)
1. Speak respectfully of parents in the presence of others
2. Use manners taught by parents with parents
3. Submit to the preferences of Parents while living with them
4. Listen respectfully to them whether they agree or disagree
5. Do not give disrespectful remarks as rebuttal to their questions
6. Respect their position on areas where they differ by not doing those things where they all differ around them

Marriage and Family

(Section Thirteen)

Dating God's Way
(1 Timothy 5:1-2)

I. Characteristics of Dating God's Way

Read: 1 Timothy 5:1-2, Romans 15:1-3, Hebrews 10:24-25, 1 Thessalonians 4:1-8, Philippians 2:3-4, James 2:1, 1 Thessalonians 5:22

If you take these passages and apply them to a biblical dating relationship here is what you will come up with:

A. People who date God's way treat the opposite sex like a brother or sister and not a husband or wife .

B. People who date God's way develop friendships that lead to Godliness.

C. People who date God's way seek to bless others and serve them according to their need.

D. People who date God's way do not obligate themselves to any one person because they are just friends not married.

E. People who date God's way treat those they are attracted to and those they are not attracted to the same way.

F. People who date God's way do things that only a brother and sister would do and nothing else.

G. People who date God's way do things with each other that they could continue to do if either of them were married to other people.

H. People who date God's way avoid all forms of sexual intimacy so that they do not defraud one another, and so they can keep the marriage bed undefiled.

I. People who date God's way do not seek to satisfy fleshy or worldly desires of one another.

J. People who date God's way do not seek to control or dictate when or who the other person can spend time with because they are friends not married.

K. People who date God's way do not break up because there is nothing to break up; they are friends instead of illegitimate lovers.

L. People who date God's way seek not to impress or entice each other but to impart truth and encourage one another .

M. People who date God's way do nothing out of fear of losing the other person because neither of them have nothing to loose nor are they seeking to use one another

II. Characteristics of Dating the World's Way

Read: 1Thessalonians 4:1-8, 2Timothy 3:1-4, Galatians 5:19-21, Proverbs 22:3, Philippians 3:17-19, Romans 8:5-7, 1John 2:14-15, 1 Corinthians 6:12-20)

If you take these passages and apply them to a worldly dating relationship here is what you will come up with:

A.   People who date the world's way have ownership over each other.

B.   People who date the world's way develop relationships that lead to sin and ungodliness.

C.   People who date the world's way are looking for someone to make them happy not help them be holy.

D.   People who date the world's way do things with each other that they would have to stop doing if either of them were married to other people.

E.   People who date the world's way engage in all kinds of sexual intimacy; they seek to satisfy any and all fleshly desires of each other.

F.   People who date the world's way do things that are designed exclusively for a husband and wife relationship.

G.   People who date the world's way seek to control or dictate with whom and how the other person can spend time with others.

H.   People who date the world's way seek to impress and entice each other in order to get what they want from each other.

I.   People who date the world's way break up because they have been together as if they were husband and wife and thus must have some formal agreement that they are no longer going to have sex with each other and treat each other as a husband or wife.

J.   People who date the world's way do many things out of fear of losing the illegitimate pleasures they are getting from the other person.

K.   People who date the world's way give preferential treatment to those they are attracted to.

L.   People who date the world's way require you to be obligated to them as you would a husband or wife.

III. The Danger of Dating the World's Way (Proverbs 14:14)

A. You establish an illegitimate covenant with someone (1Corinthians 6:12-20).

B. You defraud your brother or sister into illegitimate thoughts, words, and actions (1Thessalonians 4:1-8).

C. You arouse passions and desires that are to be reserved until marriage (Song of Solomon 3:5).

D. You put the other person in the position of being spiritually and emotionally harmed because of the illegitimate ties that form (1Corinthians 6:12-20).

E. You set yourself up to be impure going into marriage (1Corinthians 6:12-20).

F. You set yourself up to be disciplined by God (Hebrews 13:4).

G. You establish patterns of thinking about the opposite sex that are worldly instead of Godly (Matthew 5:27-28).

IV. The Benefit of Dating God's Way (Proverbs 14:15-16)

A. You will consider their interest above your own (Philippians 2:3-4).

B. You will seek their highest good not your greatest gain (Romans 15:1-2).

C. You will hang with people that will lead you into wisdom instead of worldliness (Proverbs 13:20) .

D. You help others walk in love and good deeds (Hebrew 10:19-25).

E. You help each other stay pure for marriage (Hebrews 13:4, 1 Thessalonians 4:1-8).

V. Marriage can become an option when: (1Corinthians 7:27-28)

A. Both have received wise counsel to determine if it is feasible (Proverbs 15:22).

B. Both have decided that they are willing to make a commitment to fulfill the responsibilities of being husband and wife (Ecclesiastes 5:5-6).

C. Both are equally yoked (2Corinthians 6:14-7:1).

VI. Marriage should not to become an option if: (Philippians 2:3-5)

A. Both want to get married to make each other happy (Jeremiah 17:5-9).

B. Both want to get married to gratify the flesh (1Thessalonians 4:1-8).

C. Both want to get married because they are tired being alone (Philippians 2:1-5).

Dating God's Way vs. Dating the World's Way

-Involves friendship	-Involves ownership
-Includes many friends	-Exclusive to each other
-Has no sexual intimacy	-Includes all forms of sexual
-Requires no obligation	- Requires obligation
-Focuses on holiness	- Focuses on happiness
-Seeks to bless others	- Seeks to get a blessing from others
-Seeks to impart truth to others	-Seeks to impress others
-Seeks to encourage others	-Seeks to entice others
-Supports the other's decisions	-Dictates the other's decisions
-Fear dishonoring the other	-Fear losing the other

The Danger of Sexual Immorality

I. The Plan of Sex
A. God made male and female body parts to complement each other (Genesis 1:27).
B. God designed sex for procreation of mankind to display His image and for husband and wife to enjoy one another in their union (Genesis 1:28, Song 4:15- 5:1).
C. God commanded sexual relations between male and female only (Genesis 1:28).
D. Sex is for married persons only (Hebrews 13:4).
E. Sexual desire is a normal and natural occurrence (Song of Solomon 4:15- 5:1).

II. The Perversions of Sex

A. Adultery – married persons having sexual relations outside of their own marriage (Hebrews 13:4, Proverbs 6:32).
B. Pre marital sex – single persons having sexual relations before marriage (1 Corinthians 6:15, 1 Thessalonians 4:3-5).
C. Homosexuality – persons having sex with someone of the same sex (Romans 1:24-28, Genesis, 19:1-29, 1 Corinthians 6:9-11).
D. Incest – sexual relations between persons so closely related that law or religion forbids them to marry (1 Corinthians 5:1, Leviticus 20:11-12,14).
E. Rape – the unlawful and unwanted/unconsented forcing of sexual relations (2 Samuel 13: 11-15, Deuteronomy 22:23-30, Judges 19:25, 20:3-4,12).
F. Prostitution/Harlotry – the giving or selling of one's body for sexual and/or financial profit (Proverb 23:7, Deuteronomy 23:18, 1 Corinthians 6:15-18).
G. Voyeurism – sexual stimulation and/or arousal by watching others engaged in sexual acts (Matthew 5:28, Exodus 20:17, Philippians 4:8).
F. Pornography – mental/visual stimulation caused by seeing sexual conduct or nakedness (Matthew 5:28, Exodus 20:17, Philippians 4:8).
G. Exhibitionism – the self-display of the genitals without the consent of others (Romans 13:14, Ephesians 5:1-5).
H. Bestiality – sexual contact with animals (Exodus 22:19, Leviticus 18:23, Deuteronomy 27:21).
I. Sado- Masochism – sexual excitement that is derived through personal suffering and pain; the key is the concept of a submittal to power; Sadist want to subject the victim to pain for sexual excitement; Masochists want to be subjected to the pain for sexual excitement (Galatians 5:13, Philippians 2:3-4).
(A-I was adapted from Dr. Stuart Scott from a class titled Problems and Procedures.)

III. The Pitfalls to Unlawful Sex
    A. God will judge all who have sex outside of marriage (Hebrews 13:4).

    B. God will judge all who use people as objects (sexually) to gratify their lust for pleasure and excitement (Thessalonians 4:4-6).

    C. Those who choose to have sex outside of marriage bring about destruction on themselves (Proverbs 5:1-23).

    D. Those who choose to have sex outside marriage will suffer negative consequences (Proverbs 6:23-35, 1Corinthians 6:12-20).

IV. The Process of Repenting of Unlawful Sex
    A. Identify, confess and repent of all unlawful sexual activities you are or have been participating in (1 John 1:9, Proverbs 28:13-14).

    B. Identify what lust of your heart you where trying to satisfy through the unlawful sexual activities (James 1:14-15, Philippians 3:17-19).

    C. Seek forgiveness from those individuals you have been committing sexual sin with (James 5:16, Luke 17:3).

    D. Make a commitment to please God (2 Corinthians 5:9-10, 2 Corinthians 5:15).

    E. Dwell on things that are pure (Philippians 4:8).

    F. Make no more provisions for future unlawful sexual activities (1 Corinthians 6:12-20, 1 Thessalonians 4:3-8, Romans 13:11-14).

    G. Learn how to treat older men as fathers, older women as mothers, younger men as brothers, and younger women as sisters with absolute purity (1 Timothy 5:1).

    H. Learn the art of worshiping God instead of your desires (John 4:23-24, Romans 12:1-21, Hebrews 13:15-16, Matthew 4:8-10).

MARRIAGE AND FAMILY

(Section Fourteen)

Making Friends

I. The Premise of a Friend
A. A friend is one who is intimately close to another (Proverbs 17:17).
B. A friend is one who is familiar with and connected to another in productive God honoring way (Proverbs 17:17).
C. A friend is one who is so close they become family in a good way (Proverbs 18:24).

II. The Prerequisite to a Good Friendship (being a Friend of God)
A. A friend of God has faith in Jesus Christ (James 2:23).
B. A friend of God obeys what God says (John 15:12-17).
C. A friend of God breaks away from worldliness (James 4:4-8, 1John 2:15-17).
D. A friend of God loves others as commanded by God. (John 15:12-17).

III. The Practice of a Friend
A. A friend provides support in times of trouble (Proverbs 17:17).
B. A friend tells you the truth even when it hurts (Proverbs 27:6).
C. A friend does not abandon you in time of need (Proverbs 27:10).
E. A friend is able to give and receive counsel (Proverbs 27:9).
F. A friend is willing to sacrifice his life for you (John 15:13).

IV. The Priorities of a Friend
A. A true friend should seek to lead you to be reconciled to God the Father through Christ Jesus our Lord (2Corinthians 5:11-21).
B. A true friend should lead you to belong to the community of Christ (Hebrews 10:19-25).
C. A true friend should help you to become like Christ in your character and lifestyle (Colossians 1:28-29, Ephesians 4:11-16).

V. The Principles for building a Friendship
A. Consider the interest of others above your own (Philippians 2:3-4).
B. Serve one another (1Peter 4:10).
C. Speak the truth at all times with love (Ephesians 4:15,25,29).
D. Support one another in time of need(1John 3:17-18).
E. Confront sin in the lives of others (Galatians 6:1-2).
F. Let others know when they have sinned against you (Luke 17:3).
G. Forgive others accordingly (Ephesians 4:32).
H. Be a good listener (Proverbs 20:5, Proverbs 18:13).
I. Be patient with others (1Corinthians 13:4).
J. Don't cause others to stumble (Romans 14:13-21).

K. Be kind to one another (Ephesians 4:32).

VI. The Problems that can ruin a Friendship
   A. Lacking loyalty and confidentiality (Proverbs 16:28).
   B. Confessing sin without repenting of sin (Proverbs 17:9).
   C. Insulting or disgracing a friend (Psalm 15:3).
   D. Having a bad temper (Proverbs 22:24-25).

VII. The Procedure for addressing problems in a Friendship
   A. Get the log out of your eye first (Matthew 7:3-5).
   B. Free yourself from your sin first (Proverbs 28:13-14, 1John 1:9).
   C. Confess your sins to your brother (James 5:16).
   D. Go and show your brother his faults (Luke 17:3, Proverbs 27:6).
   E. If he repents forgive him and move on in the friendship (Luke 17:3).
   F. If he does not repent take witnesses to seek to settle it (Matthew 18:15-20).
   G. If he does not repent take it to the leadership of the Church (Matthew 18:15-20).

VIII. The Particulars to discuss about Friendship
   A. What ways are you showing yourself to be a friend?
   B. Are you helping people draw close to God or are you helping them to fall away from God?
   C. Are you helping people build good friendships or are you breaking up intimate friendships?
   D. Are you helping others function as God intended?
   E. Who is receiving the benefits of your friendship?
   F. Who is not but needs to receive the benefits of your friendship?
   G. What people in your life fit the description of a friend as described above?
   H. If no one in your life fits the description what conclusions can you draw?
   I. What friendships have you broken off lately and why?
   J. What was the main thing that ruined the friendship?
   K. How did you contribute to the ruin of the friendship?
   L. Do you think the friendship can be repaired? Why or why not?

BIBLIOGRAPHY

Books

Solving Marriage Problems, Jay E. Adams, Zondervan Publishing, 1983

Mastering you Money, Ron Blue, Thomas Nelson Publishing, 1991

For A World Like Ours: Studies in 1 Corinthians, James L. Boyer, Baker Book House, 1971

Manly Dominion: In A Passive-Purple Four Ball World, Mark Chanski, Calvary Press Publishing, 2004

Safe People, Henry Cloud, John, Townsend, Zondervan Publishing House, 1995

The Mature Man: Becoming a Man of Impact Dewitt, David, Vision House Publishing Inc., 1994

At the Alter of Sexual Idolatry, Steve Gallagher Pure Life Ministries, 1986

Dating With Integrity, John Holzmann, Word Publishing, 1992

Theological Dictionary of the New Testament. Gerhard, Kittel;, Gerhard, Friedrich ; Geoffrey William Bromiley, W.B. Eerdmans, 1995

Faithful and True Sexual Integrity in a Fallen World, Mark Laaser, Life Way Press, 1996

Relationships: A Mess Worth Making, Tim Lane, New Growth Press, 2006

Real Questions, Real Answers About Sex, Dr. Louis & Melissa McBurney, Zondervan Publishers, 2005

The Myth of the Greener Grass, J. Allan Petersen, Tyndale Publishing, 1991

The Exemplary Husband, Dr. Stuart Scott, Focus Publishing, 2000

The Peacemaker, Ken Sande, Baker Books, 1997

The Heart of Man and Mental Disorders, Rich Thomson, Biblical Counseling Ministries, Inc., 2004

The War of Words, Paul Tripp, P& R Publishers, 2000

Shepherding a Child's Heart, Ted Tripp, Shepherd Press, 1995

The Master's College (Santa Clarita, Ca.) Biblical Counseling Course Material

Marriage & Family Course, Dr. Wayne Mack

Policies and Procedures Course, Dr. Stuart Scott

Tape /CD Series

The Fulfilled Family, Tape Series, John F. MacArthur

The Pursuit of Manhood: Discovering the Journey and Joys of Biblical Masculinity, Jim Berg

Shepherd's Conference Workshop, Grace Community Church 1999

Pursuing Personal Purity (Guarding your Heart), Bible Study Notes from Jim Pile

CPSIA information can be obtained
at www.ICGtesting.com
Printed in the USA
LVHW060805011221
704961LV00011B/312